SECRETS OF THE MUMMIES

Special Edition

First published in the United States by
Hyperion Books for Children
a division of the Walt Disney Company
114 Fifth Avenue
New York, NY 10011-5690
3 5 7 9 10 8 6 4 2

Library of Congress Cataloging-in-Publication Data
Tanaka, Shelley.

Secrets of the mummies: uncovering the bodies of ancient Egyptians / by Shelley Tanaka;
illustrations by Greg Ruhl; historical consultation by Peter Brand.
p.   cm.

Summary: Describes the ancient Egyptian practice of preserving the dead through the process of mummification and
explains what scientists have learned from unwrapping and examining mummies.

ISBN 0-7868-1539-6
1. Mummies — Egypt Juvenile literature. 2. Egypt — Civilization — To 332 B.C. Juvenile literature.
[1. Mummies. 2. Egypt — Civilization — To 332 B.C.] I. Ruhl, Greg, ill. II. Title.
DT62.M7T36 1999
393'.0932—dc21   99-11012
CIP

Produced by
Madison Press Books
40 Madison Avenue
Toronto, Ontario
Canada M5R 2S1

Printed in Singapore

SECRETS OF THE MUMMIES

Uncovering the bodies of ancient Egyptians

BY SHELLEY TANAKA

ILLUSTRATIONS BY GREG RUHL

Historical consultation by Dr. Peter Brand

A HYPERION/MADISON PRESS BOOK

Prologue

The room is dark, even though it is early afternoon. Heavy curtains have been pulled across the tall windows, blocking out light and noise from the busy city street outside. The parlor is dimly lit with candles and gas lamps that throw eerie shadows against the high ceilings.

The guests are waiting, their voices hushed. Some pull watches out of their pockets to check the time. The invitation said the mummy would be unrolled at half past two.

On one side of the room, doors open. A butler wheels in a table. A long wooden box sits on top of it. The box is open.

The crowd leans over expectantly. A few hang back. They have heard the stories about mummy unwrappings — the dead insects that fall to the floor as the bandages are removed, the limbs, suddenly released from their bindings, that slowly rise into the air, as if alive.

And then, the sight of that ancient face, uncovered for the first time in more than three thousand years....

The Mummy Hunters

Once a living being is dead, its body begins to decay. Gradually, the soft parts rot away or are eaten by insects, until only the bones and teeth are left. Over time, even these will crumble away to nothing.

If this decomposition process can be stopped, you end up with a preserved corpse — a mummy.

Throughout history, in many different parts of the world, people have wanted to preserve their dead. In Chile, people created mummies more than one thousand years before the Egyptians did. They removed the insides from the bodies, dried and stuffed them, coated them with clay, and fitted them with wigs. In Alaska, ancient people dried and stuffed the bodies of their leaders, believing they could then continue to be consulted for

(Opposite) One of the three giant pyramids at Giza built by the pharaohs as resting places for their mummies. (Above) A gilded mummy mask was intended to help a person's spirit identify its body.

advice. There are also mummies that have been preserved by accident — in bogs, ice, caves, or buried in sand.

Most of the mummies that we know about, however, come from Egypt. They were made three to four thousand years ago, and many have been discovered during the past two hundred years. For the Egyptians, mummy making was an exact and serious art. It was an important part of their beliefs, and it said a great deal about how they viewed their world and their lives.

The Egyptians believed that a person's spirit lived on after death. During the day, the spirit would leave the body and fly freely around the next world. But at night, it had to return to its tomb in the present world. Unless the body was kept looking lifelike, the spirit would not recognize it. (Many mummies were given masks, and coffins had faces painted on them to help the spirit recognize its earthly home.)

Why are they called Mummies?

Some of the earliest mummies that were discovered appeared to be covered with bitumen, or pitch, a tarlike substance that becomes shiny and hard when it dries. The Arabic word for bitumen is *mumia*, so people began to call these preserved bodies "mummies." In fact, the blackened mummies were covered with resin — plant gum — that had darkened over the centuries.

To remain whole, a body had to be protected from the things that caused it to decompose: air, moisture, and insects. First, embalmers removed the large internal organs: the brain, lungs, stomach, liver, and intestines. (These soft, wet tissues decompose more quickly than any other body parts.) Then they packed and covered the body with a kind of salt, called natron, which would dry it out. Finally, they covered the mummy with resin and wrapped it in bandages, usually placing jewelry and charms

Mummies were often buried inside a coffin (right) or a nested set of coffins (left) decorated with images of gods and goddesses, scenes from the mummy's journey to the next world, and written spells for protection from evil.

between the layers of cloth to protect the body in the afterlife. The wrapped mummy would be placed in a coffin (sometimes several coffins nested within each other) and buried in a tomb deep in the earth. And there it was supposed to rest, undisturbed, forever.

In fact, the mummies did not rest peacefully for long. Robbers soon broke into the tombs to steal from the graves and tear apart the mummies for their jewelry and amulets. And even once the valuable items had been removed, the mummies were still not left in peace.

Eight hundred years ago, it was thought that bitumen, a black tarlike substance made from oil and minerals, could be used as medicine. The resins that were used to cover mummies had made many of them turn black, as if they were covered with bitumen. It wasn't long before people decided that mummies themselves contained bitumen. Mummies were dug out of their tombs and ground into powder. The powder was used to try to cure everything from coughs and stomachaches to bruises and broken bones. Sometimes mummies were boiled to make ointments to put on cuts.

In fact, mummies contained no bitumen, and swallowing mummy often caused vomiting, stomach cramps, and bad breath. But that didn't stop people from wanting it. Even the king of France used mummy, mixed with a little mashed rhubarb, to treat his ailments.

And there were more insults in store for these bodies that had once been so carefully preserved. For European tourists in the nineteenth century, a mummy unwrapping was a highlight of an Egyptian vacation. Some took the mummies back home as souvenirs.

This scene from about 1880 shows an Egyptian guarding a group of mummies, most likely collected as souvenirs for tourists.

Friends were then invited to come and view the unwrapping.

Although the event would be advertised as an unrolling, usually the bandages, hardened with ancient resin, had to be cut or chiseled off. Spectators would gather, filled with nervous anticipation. Would jewels and gold fall out of the bandages — or just dead beetles? Would the mouth be gaping open in horror or smiling in peace? Would the mummy be a man or a woman? Young or old? Dry and crumbly

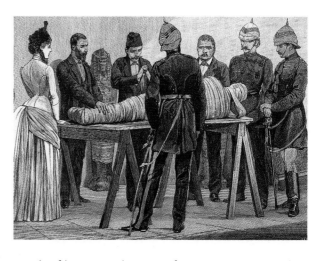

(Left) A British poster from 1842 invites the public to view two mummies just brought from Egypt. (Above) Public mummy unwrappings allowed many people to look at mummies, but the ancient bodies were never properly studied before they were thrown away.

Wrapping the Mummy

An Egyptian mummy was always wrapped in cloth before being placed in its coffin. Sometimes thin strips of linen were wound around the body in complicated patterns, followed by larger sheets, held in place by thin bands. In later mummies, paintings of the deceased were sometimes placed over the wrapped body's head, as with the two mummies of children at left.

Sometimes all these bandages hid the work of a careless embalmer. Embalming workshops were busy places, with many bodies being prepared at once. An unidentified ear or limb might be hastily tucked into the bandages of the closest mummy, with no one the wiser.

or hard and shiny? What would it smell like? Sweet, like most mummies?

People would shiver as they recalled other unrollings they had heard about. The mummy that had an arrowhead sticking out of its skull. The mummy that held the corpse of a tiny baby. The mummy whose feet had been broken off so the body would fit into the coffin. The mummy that had artificial toes made from reeds and mud. The mummy that must have been nibbled by two mice, which were then accidentally wrapped up with it, their tiny skeletons now remaining between the bandages.

Sometimes a doctor or Egyptian expert was on hand to explain the finds, to turn the event into an educational experience. But generally not much was learned that was useful from a scientific point of view. Once the body had been uncovered and everyone had had a good look, the mummy was usually tossed into the garbage.

That wasn't the end of uses for mummies. Many were sold as antiques, to be collected by the rich, like an old vase or piece of sculpture. Others were ground up to make brown wrapping paper. Some were even used as fuel for trains.

It's estimated that the Egyptians prepared hundreds of thousands of mummies. Given the many ways they have been used, it is amazing that any survived. But some did. At the same time, we have become smarter and more respectful in the way we treat mummies. In fact, we have learned that mummies have a great deal to tell us — both about the ancient Egyptians and about ourselves.

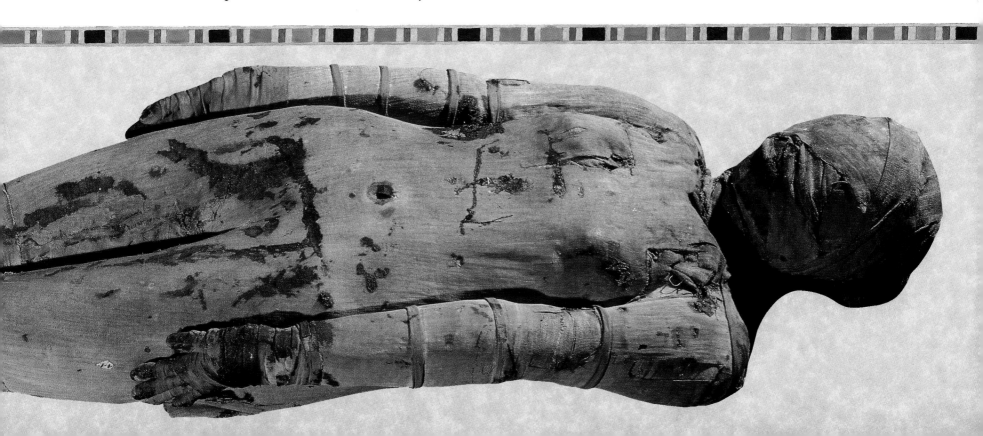

Unwrapping the Mummy

It was not easy to preserve one's body and belongings for eternity. But if anyone could do this, it was the pharaohs — the kings of ancient Egypt. They had the power and wealth to command whatever they wished.

The early pharaohs built enormous pyramids, which served both as their tombs and as monuments to their greatness. But these pyramids were like giant billboards in the desert, advertising the buried treasure that lay beneath them. Before long, determined thieves robbed the tombs of their riches.

Later kings had tombs built deep underground in a remote, barren valley nestled beneath steep cliffs. This valley came to be known as the Valley of the Kings. The entrances were carefully sealed and heavily guarded. Yet eventually these burial places were robbed, too, often by the families of the original builders. Entire villages would make their living from tomb robbery, passing the secrets of their trade from generation to generation.

As tomb after tomb was emptied of its treasure, little could be done except to try to save the bodies of the dead.

(Opposite) The mummy of Ramses II. (Above) Four colossal statues of Ramses II sit at the entrance to Abu Simbel, a temple the pharaoh had carved out of a solid rock cliff.

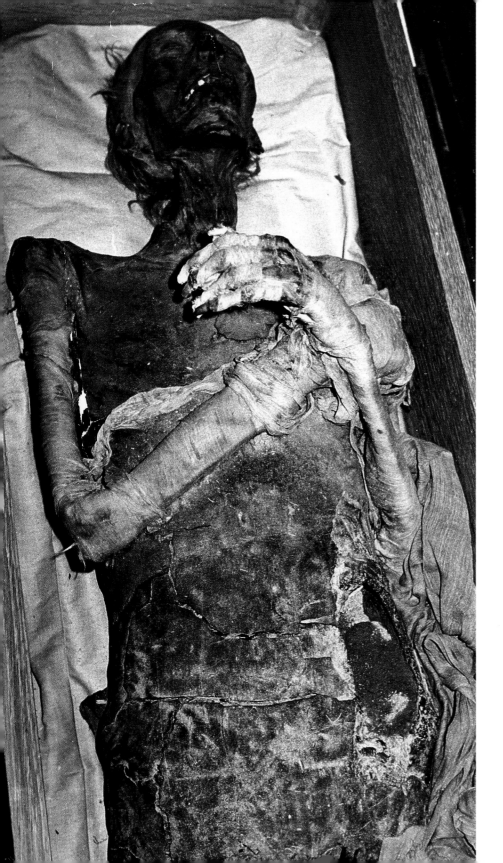

Priests would secretly transport the mummies from one hiding place to another, in an attempt to outwit the thieves. In spite of their best efforts, however, most of these locations were discovered before too long.

Only a few hiding places remained undisturbed. It took three thousand years before one of the biggest of these was found.

In 1881, as many as forty royal mummies were found packed in an unmarked chamber cut deep into the cliffs above the Valley of the Kings. The most famous among them was Ramses II, known as Ramses the Great. During his long reign, he built more temples and monuments and fathered more children than any other pharaoh in history.

Thieves had removed any gold and precious stones from the body and coffin long before. But experts were anxious to examine the mummy itself. As pharaoh, Ramses had likely received the most elaborate funeral preparations available at the time. What condition would the body be in? What would it reveal about how the Egyptians mummified their dead?

Officials quickly cut through the bandages from head to foot. And suddenly they were staring into the face of a king.

It was clear that the ancient embalmers had done their work well. Ramses had been at least eighty-five years old when he died. But even stripped of his golden

To restore the pharaoh's dried body to its original shape, the embalmers stuffed it with linen, bits of wood, and flower bulbs.

funeral mask and other treasures, he looked like a king. His skin was close to its natural color, not blackened with resin. The embalmers had even dyed his hair red to make him look more youthful.

Most impressive of all was his face. The profile was strong and noble, the skull perfectly intact. This was no small achievement, given that Ramses' entire brain had been removed.

Removing the brain was a normal part of the mummification process. But getting it out without destroying the head or face was a delicate operation.

Over the years, embalmers found that the easiest route into the skull was through the nose.

Using various hooks and knives inserted through the nostrils, they would gently poke around and break up the brain. Then they used small scoops and water to flush out the pieces.

Once his brain had been removed, the inside of Ramses' skull was filled with liquid resin. Animal bones and peppercorns were stuffed into his nose to restore its natural shape and awaken his sense of smell in the next world.

As officials continued to examine the pharaoh's body, they found a large incision on the left side of the abdomen, where embalmers had removed the stomach, lungs, liver, and intestines. But these organs had not simply been thrown away. Each one was carefully dried

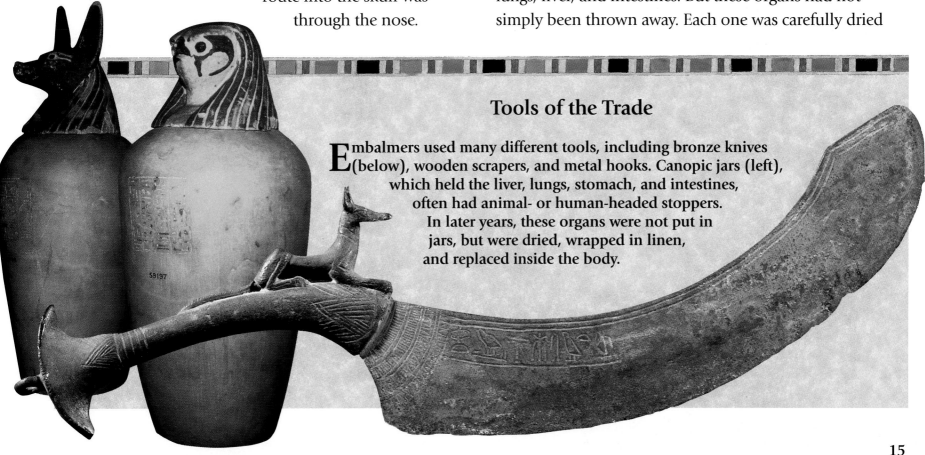

Tools of the Trade

Embalmers used many different tools, including bronze knives (below), wooden scrapers, and metal hooks. Canopic jars (left), which held the liver, lungs, stomach, and intestines, often had animal- or human-headed stoppers. In later years, these organs were not put in jars, but were dried, wrapped in linen, and replaced inside the body.

59197

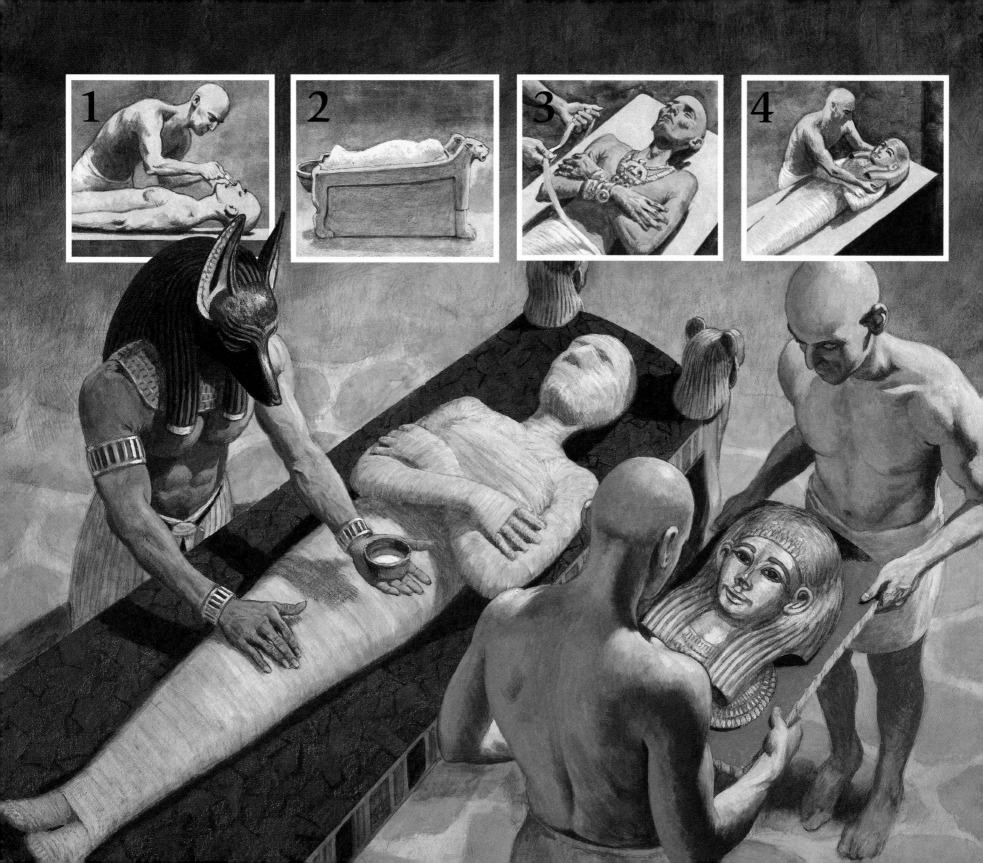

Making a Mummy

There were many ways to make a mummy, but the basic method remained the same: the body was dried, then wrapped and decorated. The whole process could take as long as seventy days, and each stage was overseen by special priests.

1 The stomach, liver, intestines, and lungs were removed through an incision in the abdomen. The brain was removed through the nostrils, using special hooks and spoons. Unlike the other organs, which were carefully dried and wrapped, the brain was thought to be of no importance and was thrown away.

2 The entire body was stuffed and covered with natron, a kind of powdered salt, and placed on a slanted table. The salt dissolved the fats in the body and released the liquids, which were collected in a container and buried.

3 After about thirty to forty days, the salt was removed. The dried, shrunken body was rubbed with perfume, then washed with milk and wine and covered with resin. The inside of the body, along with the eye sockets and nostrils, were stuffed with linen, mud, or reeds to help them keep their shape. The body was then decorated with jewelry and magic amulets and carefully wrapped in up to twenty layers of cloth.

4 The mummy's head was often covered with a mask of the deceased, so that the spirit could recognize it. Then the mummy was placed in a mummy case.

with natron and washed with palm wine and spices, then wrapped in linen. The organs were either put back into the body or, as in the case of Ramses, placed in their own miniature coffins. These coffins were then laid in a special stone box called a canopic chest. (The heart, which was thought to be the source of a person's intelligence and feeling, was always left in the body.)

A priest wearing a mask of Anubis, the jackal-headed god of embalming, puts the finishing touches on a mummy. Wrapped mummies were often placed on lion-shaped couches like the one shown in this wall painting.

The rest of the body hollow would be washed, sometimes with long swabs that reached up into the chest. The abdomen would be stuffed with cloth, sand, sawdust, mud, or even onions, to dry it out and help it keep its shape. A sheet of gold had likely covered the hole in Ramses' belly, but this had long since been stolen by grave robbers.

Once the insides had been prepared, the whole body would be placed on a slanted table and covered with a pile of natron. Over several weeks, blood and body fluids would run out, and the skin and muscles

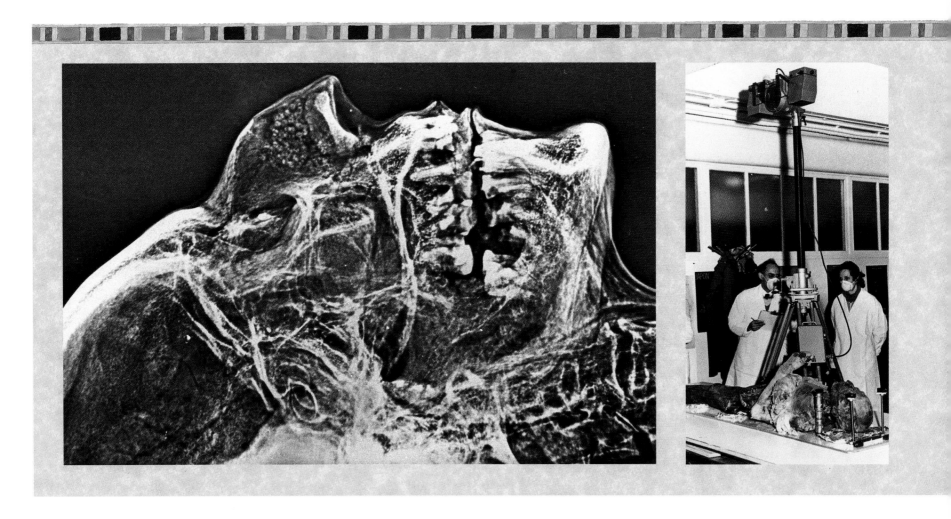

would turn dry. When the body was completely dry, it would be rubbed with perfumes, spices, resins, and oils. The perfumes and spices gave it a sweet smell. The resins acted as a glue and sealer, and they disinfected the body, to stop destructive bacteria from growing. Oils, or sometimes even wine or milk, were massaged into the skin to soften it.

Finally, the body would be carefully wrapped in hundreds of yards of cloth, every finger and toe bound separately. This bandaging was an important part of Egyptian mummification, though cloth was not always easy to come by, since it was all woven by hand. Kings were wrapped in the finest linen, specially prepared by expert weavers. Poorer people were bound in strips of old cloth, such as worn-out sails from ships. The bandaging procedure alone could take two weeks.

Back in the 1880s, there was a limit to what scientists could learn from the mummy of Ramses.

Careful study by scientists (left) revealed that Ramses' kingly profile was enhanced by a small bone used to prop open his nostrils, and that his nose was stuffed with peppercorns to help reawaken his sense of smell (far left). Though he was in his eighties when he died, Ramses still had much of his hair (top right). His carefully wrapped fingers (bottom right) show the skill of his embalmers.

So once the body had been unwrapped, poked, and prodded, it was replaced in its coffin and put on display in a museum in Cairo.

The mummy had remained perfectly preserved for more than three thousand years. Now, stripped of its cocoon of bandages, it was exposed to the air. Even tucked away in a glass case, it slowly began to deteriorate.

In 1974, museum officials noticed that something was eating the mummy's neck. It turned out to be beetle larvae. Insects help dead bodies decompose. Now here they were, thousands of years later, busily doing their work. Unless they were stopped, the great Egyptian king's body would soon be nothing but dust.

The decision was made to send Ramses II to experts in Paris, where the body was examined and sterilized, using radiation. Like all heads of state, Ramses was welcomed by a full military salute and honor guard. He even had a passport — Occupation: King (deceased).

By the 1970s, scientists were able to learn far more about the old king's health. Using X rays and small surgical microscopes, they discovered that the pharaoh had had ailments that still plague the elderly today. He'd had arthritis and bad teeth. And, like other Egyptian mummies that have been examined recently, he'd suffered from heart disease. Heart disease is considered by many to be a modern problem, caused or worsened by things like smoking, stress, a high-fat diet, and lack of exercise. Yet the ancient Egyptians suffered from it, too. Scientists will continue to try to find out why and how this might help us control the disease today.

Ramses II lived more than twice as long as the average Egyptian male. By the time he died, he was a frail old man. He probably had difficulty moving and chewing. He may have had cramps in his legs and feet and probably walked with a bit of a limp. He was likely in constant pain during the last years of his life.

What was it like for these ancient people when they became sick or old? Their mummies may help us learn the answers.

The Story of Ramses II

He ruled the most powerful nation in the world. But he knew that a great king should always be on the minds of his people. So over the years of his long reign, he built dozens of grand monuments and temples to celebrate his importance. There were gigantic statues carved out of cliffs. His temple at Karnak was the glory of Egypt, its magnificent painted columns rising like fists to the sky. He constructed huge canals, glittering palaces, entire towns. For years, he had been building his own tomb in the Valley of the Kings, an underground palace of treasuries, chariot halls, large corridors, and a grand burial vault.

Even other buildings were rededicated in his honor. On his orders the carvings and names of the former rulers who had built them were chiseled away. New murals were put in their places, deeply carved into the stone, so they could not be erased so easily by future kings. They showed scenes of Ramses in his chariot, his tame lion at his side as he led his army into battle or stormed the strongholds of the enemy. Even though he had not fought all of these battles himself, it is true that he'd assembled one of the largest armies the world had ever seen, with lines of soldiers stretching for miles as they rode into war.

At home in his huge palaces, he surrounded himself with scholars, generals, and scribes, as well as his many wives and one hundred children. He took his eldest sons into battle when they were small. They remained well back of the front lines, to be sure, and heavily guarded by their personal charioteers, but he wanted to give them a taste of their destiny as future pharaohs. He was building a dynasty and he knew the importance of family.

Under his reign, Egypt was a wealthy empire, respected and feared. Countries he had conquered kept the royal treasury filled with a steady supply of slaves, ivory, incense, weapons, precious woods, and leopard skins. Gold poured in from the mines he had built in neighboring Nubia.

He ruled for sixty-six years and outlived his twelve oldest sons, as well as many of their younger brothers and sisters. When he died in the summer of 1213 B.C., the royal barge carried his body up the Nile to his burial site, a three-week journey. Mourners lined the banks of the river and wailed as they watched the coffin glide by.

If the gods were willing, the world would not forget their great pharaoh and the glory he had brought to Egypt.

Treasures for the Afterlife

By the end of the nineteenth century, the supply of mummies, especially royal mummies, was shrinking. Most of the tombs of the great Egyptian kings had been found, and every single one had already been robbed.

Still, a few stubborn adventurers insisted that there was more to discover.

For several years, an English archaeologist named Howard Carter had been searching the Valley of the Kings for the tomb of Tutankhamen, a young pharaoh of ancient Egypt. But by 1922, time was running out. Lord Carnarvon, who was providing the money for the search, had decided not to pay for another season.

Carter begged for one last chance. He even said he would pay for the season's dig himself if he found nothing by the end of it.

Carter knew that there was only one small area of the valley that had not yet been thoroughly searched, because it was covered with rubble from earlier digs. So he set out to learn what lay beneath it. A long line of men and boys, each one paid a shilling a day to work from sunrise to

Howard Carter and Lord Carnarvon

Lord Carnarvon (right), a wealthy Englishman, had been told by his doctors that a hot, dry climate would be best for his health. On a trip to Egypt, he began to study archaeology, but soon realized that he'd need someone with more knowledge and experience to assist him. He was introduced to Howard Carter (left), an English archaeologist who shared Carnarvon's belief that there might be one royal tomb left undiscovered in the Valley of the Kings. Carter's skill, combined with Carnarvon's money, was to produce one of the most spectacular archaeological finds in history (opposite).

sunset, removed rock and sand, one basketful at a time.

On November 4, 1922, less than one week after the digging had begun, Carter arrived at the site to find that his team had stopped working. The men stared at him silently. He knew instantly that something unusual had happened.

The workers had found a staircase buried under the sand. There were sixteen steps in all, and they led to a doorway. Sixteen narrow steps. Could this really be the entrance to the tomb of a king?

Carter was itching to open the door. But he knew that Lord Carnarvon should share in the discovery. So he carefully filled in the stairway, making it look as if nothing had ever been found. Then he sent a telegram to England, asking Carnarvon to come right away.

Lord Carnarvon came as quickly as he could, but in those days, "right away" meant a one-week trip by car, train, ferry, ship, and donkey. When he finally arrived, the workers uncovered the doorway again. Behind it lay a rubble-filled passage. At the end of that was another door marked with the seal of Tutankhamen.

Carter chipped a hole in the door, stuck a candle through, and peered in.

"Can you see anything?" asked Carnarvon.

"Yes," replied Carter. "Wonderful things!" Later he described how the hot air escaping from the tomb had made his candle flame flicker. Then his eyes gradually grew accustomed to the light: "...details of the room within emerged slowly from the mist: strange animals,

(Left) Under Howard Carter's supervision, Egyptian laborers removed sand, gravel, and rocks by the basketful from the last unexplored area of the Valley of the Kings. Soon they had uncovered a mysterious staircase (right) with a plaster-covered doorway at the bottom.

statues, and gold — everywhere the glint of gold."

Three golden couches carved in the shapes of monstrous animals threw terrifying shadows on the wall behind them. Two life-size statues of the king, cobras snaking from their foreheads, guarded the far wall. The room was filled with glittering boxes and chests, vases, furniture, and baskets.

Carter fought the urge to plunge into the room, lift the lid off every box, peer into every basket, touch every treasure. He knew that finding the tomb was a huge responsibility. Every object had to be carefully photographed, mapped, drawn, cleaned, conserved, documented, and cataloged. (It took as long as a week just to coat one wooden object with wax so it could be transported without breaking into pieces.)

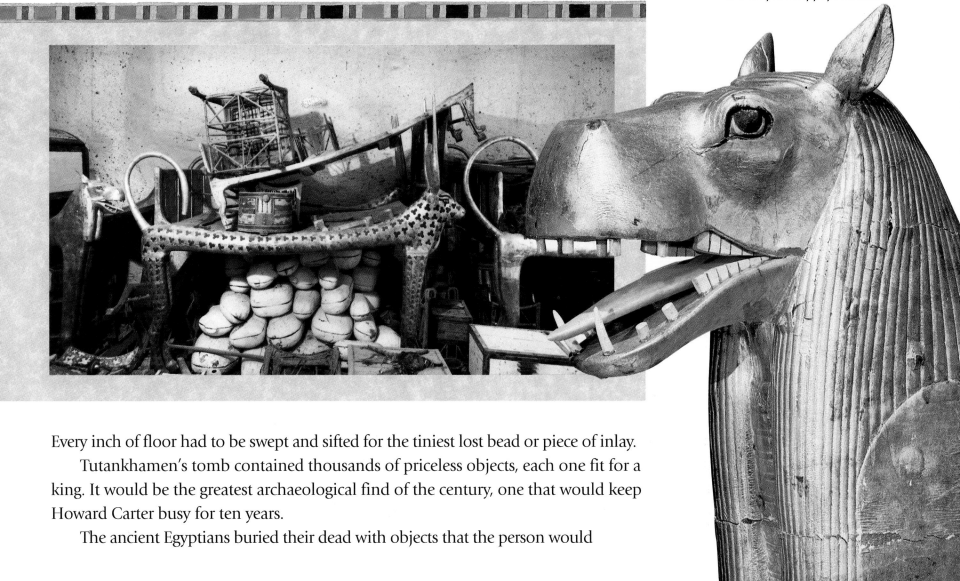

(Left) The jumble of boxes, furniture, and statues in the tomb was evidence that thieves had visited in ancient times. But among the treasures left untouched were three golden couches in the shape of animals. One of them had the head of the goddess Ammut (below), who was part crocodile, part lioness, and part hippopotamus.

Every inch of floor had to be swept and sifted for the tiniest lost bead or piece of inlay.

Tutankhamen's tomb contained thousands of priceless objects, each one fit for a king. It would be the greatest archaeological find of the century, one that would keep Howard Carter busy for ten years.

The ancient Egyptians buried their dead with objects that the person would

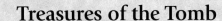

Treasures of the Tomb

The Egyptians believed that in the afterlife a person would need to use many of the objects they had owned while alive. Tutankhamen's tomb was filled with treasures fit for a pharaoh. (Top left) Guarding one room of the tomb was an elegant statue of Anubis, the jackal god of embalming. Tutankhamen's crook and flail (top right), the symbols of his kingship, were found in the tomb, along with his golden throne (below). A model boat made of alabaster had ibex heads at the front and back topped with real ibex horns (below left). Like many wealthy young men of his time, Tutankhamen wore earrings (below center) and enjoyed playing board games (bottom). A life-size statue of Tutankhamen (right) was meant to provide a home for the king's spirit in case anything were to happen to his mummy.

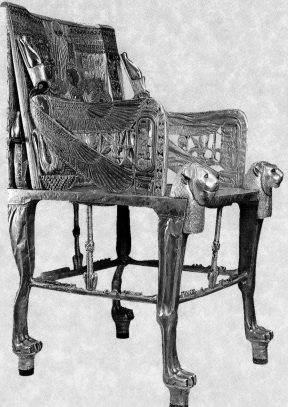

require in their afterlife — a life not that much different from the earthly one. Even the very poor were often supplied with a pot or two to take to the next world. A king, however, had a lot to pack.

There were beds, chairs, couches, and a throne inlaid with gold. Bouquets of flowers. Chariots, weapons, tools, and game boards. There were dishes and cups and mummified roast ducks and haunches of meat placed in their own little coffins. There were loaves of bread, garlic, chickpeas and lentils, honey, spices, fruit, and wine. Candlesticks and lamps had been provided to light Tutankhamen's journey through the underworld, along with statues of gods to guide him, and boats and oars to carry him. There were sandals, blankets, and underwear, makeup, mirrors, and shaving equipment, and vases filled with precious oils and perfumes. Hundreds of miniature figures of the king (called ushabtis) stood by to take his place when the gods required him to work in the fields or carry earth in the next world.

There were also personal objects from the pharaoh's past life: a small chair and toys from his childhood, a lock of his grandmother's hair, the crook and flail (symbols of kingship) that he had probably carried at his coronation.

And there were the tiny mummies of two baby girls — most likely the king's daughters.

Finally, in a separate chamber, Carter found the dead pharaoh himself.

It was clear that the ancients had wanted to make sure their king would never be disturbed, for his body was well protected. First Carter saw a gold-covered wooden shrine as big as a room. Inside it were three more large heavy shrines, also covered with gold, each one nestled inside the other. Inside the last box lay a massive sarcophagus carved from a single piece of stone. The lid alone weighed more than one ton.

In October 1923, the heavy stone lid was lifted. The officials who had gathered around gasped as two ancient linen sheets were rolled back to reveal a magnificent gold coffin fashioned in the image of the king. When the coffin lid was raised, a second gold coffin came to view, and

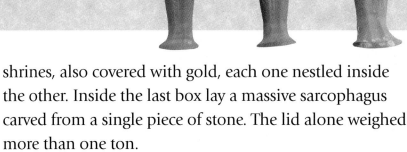

Ushabti Figures

The Egyptians believed that in the afterlife, every person — even the pharaoh — would be asked to work for the god Osiris. So that the dead didn't have to do this work, they were supplied with tiny figures called ushabtis. The word means "one who answers." These statues would magically respond when Osiris called.

Fit for a King

Tutankhamen's first two coffins were made of wood covered with a thin layer of beaten gold. His innermost coffin was made of solid gold. The king's mummy was decorated with gold bands, a beautiful gold mask, and false hands made of sheet gold.

within that lay a third coffin. This one was made of solid gold, and it weighed almost three hundred pounds.

Inside the third coffin lay the body of the young king. His head was covered with a golden mask, which many archaeologists say is the most beautiful object ever found anywhere. He wore gold sandals on his feet. His toes and fingers were covered with gold caps.

Examining the mummy was awkward and difficult. The mask and body were glued to the bottom of the coffin with the gummy resins that had been poured over them. A beaded cap was stuck to the king's head, and an intricate beaded collar lay crumbling on his chest.

In the middle of the Egyptian desert, Carter did what he had to do to remove the king's priceless mask and jewelry. He tried to melt the resins by placing the open coffin under the searing desert sun. He chiseled away chunks of linen bandages, using hot knives. He separated the king's limbs, in order to remove the 143 bracelets, daggers, and amulets that covered every part of the body.

(Above) Carter and an assistant examine the pharaoh's third coffin. (Left) Inside they would find a mummy wearing a spectacular gold mask in the image of the boy king.

By the time he was finished, there was little left of Tutankhamen but a cracked, brittle skeleton. Carter reassembled the body as best he could and laid it on a bed of sand so it could be photographed. Then the mummy was replaced in its outer

(Above) Once Carter had removed the wrappings, there was little left of Tutankhamen's body. (Left) Holes from the earrings Tutankhamen once wore can still be seen in his ears.

coffin and stone sarcophagus.

Since Carter's first examination, X rays have been taken to try to learn how the king died. Scientists could find no evidence of disease, but there was damage to the mummy's head, and the front of the rib cage was missing. No one knows whether these had anything to do with the young pharaoh's death.

King Tutankhamen's jewelry, mask, two inner coffins, and other grave goods are now displayed in museums, where they have been admired by millions of people. The treasures have been cleaned and buffed so they gleam like new. Everyone agrees they are breathtakingly beautiful.

But the king himself lies naked in his original tomb in the Valley of the Kings. Three thousand years ago, he was carefully wrapped and buried in layers of gold and stone, preserved for eternity. Now his body is slowly deteriorating. His skin is turning blacker. Bits are gradually crumbling to dust.

Even scientists feel uncomfortable about what has happened to him. Surely, some say, there must be a better way to learn from mummies.

The Story of Tutankhamen

His life was sheltered and easy from the beginning, because he was destined to be king. Servants washed, dressed, and fed him. Tutors told him what he needed to know about his country's past battles and how he would one day lead Egypt to further greatness. Priests taught him to worship the ancient sun god, Amun-Re.

His wife was chosen for him, too, and they were married when they were still children. He became king when he was only nine. Generals and priests advised him, and he followed their instructions as he always had.

To fill his days he went hunting. He would seek out hippopotamuses in the marshy areas of the Nile, pursuing them with harpoons until they were weak from loss of blood and could be pulled onto the riverbank and killed. From his hunting stool he would aim his arrows at flocks of geese or pintail ducks. When they fell from the sky, he sent his servants splashing out into the water to fetch them. But best of all was the chariot hunt. What a magnificent sight the young king made as his horse-drawn chariot and trained hounds thundered across the desert after lions or ostriches.

The rest of the time, however, there was little to do. He played board games with his wife and servants. For special celebrations like the beautiful festival of Opet, he would be pulled down the Nile on an elaborately decorated barge. Priests and soldiers marched along the riverbank, while children threw lotus flowers and the crowds cheered.

Then tragedy struck. When he was still a teenager, Tutankhamen died. But how could one so protected meet such an untimely death?

Some say it was murder, plotted by those closest to him, who were anxious to be pharaoh themselves. Maybe he was simply the victim of an unfortunate accident — a fall from a chariot while hunting, perhaps. Or he may simply have died a natural death. In those days, disease killed many, both young and old.

In any event, his death was sudden and unexpected. There was no time to prepare a burial chamber fit for a king. In the end, his tomb was barely big enough to hold all the things Tutankhamen might need in his glorious afterlife, but it would have to do. Perhaps thieves would not bother with a tomb so small. With any luck, the king could lie undisturbed there, forever.

The Mummies' Secrets

As people realized that the supply of mummies was dwindling, they began to take more care with the ones that were left. Museums around the world discussed how to treat the mummies that remained in their collections. Was it a good idea to unwrap them and open them up? Should they be put on display? Was it even right for museums to keep mummies that may have been stolen or smuggled out of Egypt in the first place?

Some argued that mummies should be examined only by X ray, which allows scientists to study the bones and location of organs in a body without cutting it open. Others said that opening up mummies could provide important information about the health of the ancient Egyptians.

The Royal Ontario Museum in Toronto, Canada, had in its collection the mummy of a young man named Nakht. X rays of his bones and teeth showed that he was just a teenager when he died. Certain lines on the ends of his bones suggested that illness or starvation may have

(Above) Nakht's simple wooden coffin was likely the best his parents could afford.
(Left) Scientists begin to remove the wrappings from the mummy.

How the Other Half Lived

Though the pharaohs are famous for their riches, most ancient Egyptians led simpler lives. The village of Deir el-Medina (above) housed the workers who built the royal tombs in the Valley of the Kings. Scribes, sculptors, and stoneworkers lived here, along with painters and carpenters. Coffins made by carpenters in Deir el-Medina were often sold to other villages, so it is possible that Nakht's coffin might have come from this town. (Left) A modest middle-class tomb. (Right) Jewelers at work.

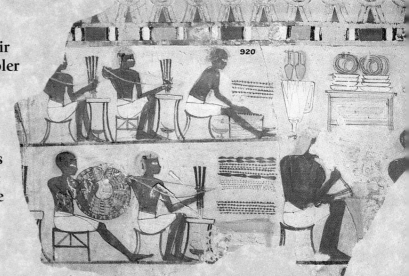

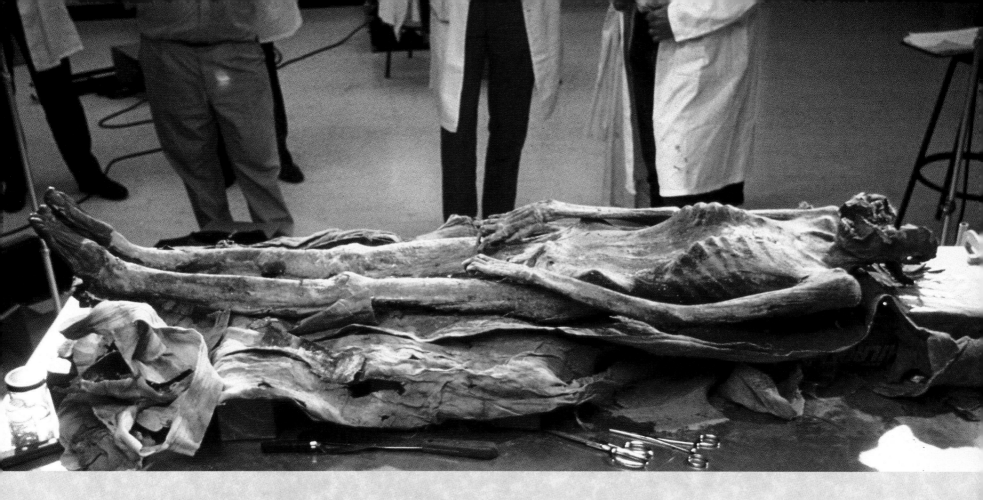

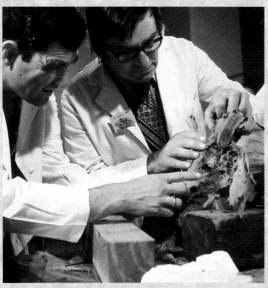

(Above) Nakht's family had him wrapped in scraps of linen, but they were probably too poor to pay for an embalmer to mummify him. His body had been naturally preserved by the hot, dry Egyptian climate, with all his internal organs still inside. (Far left and left) This gave scientists a chance to examine his liver and lungs. (Right) Nakht's skull.

stopped his growth from time to time during the last two years of his life.

X rays also showed that, unlike those of most other mummies, Nakht's brain and internal organs had never been removed. Scientists were anxious to look at these organs more closely.

The inscription on Nakht's simple wooden coffin identified him as a weaver. Mummies of laborers were rare, since only the rich could usually afford to spend so much money preparing for the afterlife. Museum officials decided that an autopsy might reveal something about how common people lived and died in Egypt thousands of years ago.

parasites, including tapeworm. Parasites have plagued people throughout history, and in ancient times there were few remedies. Nakht likely got tapeworm from eating undercooked pork. Hooked onto the lining of the intestines, a tapeworm can grow to a huge length by

Weavers at Work

Weaving was originally done by women, who had to crouch over looms that lay on the ground (left). By Nakht's time, men had entered the profession and worked on upright looms. Women also worked as basketmakers, musicians, dancers, and even in the marketplace — but most craftspeople were men.

In 1974, Nakht's body was unwrapped. The front of the chest was cut open with a saw and pried apart. Scientists were able to study the internal organs while they were in the body, as well as taking small pieces to be tested in a laboratory.

They saw that Nakht's lungs contained particles of sand and were black, probably from inhaling desert sand and smoke. And under a microscope, they found in his intestines and in his liver, kidneys, and bladder, evidence of

absorbing the food the person has eaten. The result would have been stomach pain, hunger, and loss of weight.

Laboratory tests also showed that Nakht suffered from malaria, a disease transmitted to humans by mosquitoes. It may have been this disease that killed him. In spite of all the medical advances we have made in three thousand years, in some areas we have not progressed far enough. Malaria is still one of the biggest causes of sickness and death in the world.

The Story of Nakht

He was slight and thin for a boy of fourteen, but there were many children like him. Lately the Nile's waters had been low, the crops thin. For two winters now, there hadn't been enough to eat.

Still, Nakht considered himself lucky. Many boys his age had been doing military service or working in the fields since they were ten years old. They were no better than slaves.

Nakht was a weaver, a crafter of fine linen. He was good at it, too. The blue-striped borders of his cloth were straight and elegant. His craft would provide well for the wife and children he hoped to have soon.

In the meantime, he and his family shared a simple three-room house made of mud bricks. The thin slits high in the walls helped keep out some of the heat, sand, and dust that the winds from the south blew into every nook and cranny. But the smoke from the oil lamps and his mother's cooking lingered in the stuffy, airless rooms. On hot nights, he would climb a ladder and sleep on the flat earth roof.

The heat was merciless in the desert. Yet lately, even in the blistering sun of midday, Nakht would be overcome with trembling chills, followed by a fever that made his eyes burn. His arms would feel like water, his head would ache, and he would suddenly be too weak to work at his loom. By evening he would feel better, but the chills would return the next day.

Then there was the pain in his lower belly, sometimes sharp enough to make him buckle over in agony. His mother frowned with worry when she noticed the perspiration beaded on his forehead and saw him clutching his stomach in his sleep.

When Nakht died, his parents were overcome with grief. His mother and the neighbor women wailed in the street, pulling their hair and rubbing mud into their clothes. Nakht's father could not afford to have his son prepared for the afterlife in the manner of kings. There was no money for embalming, but there would be a sturdy wooden coffin brightly painted with a fine picture of his son in a long wig.

The coffin cost more than the family earned in one month, but it was worth the expense. To lose a precious son, that was something to bring to the attention of the gods. Perhaps they would watch over him more carefully in the next world.

The autopsy of Nakht revealed a great deal about how an Egyptian worker lived and how he may have died. But once the scientists had removed Nakht's body from the coffin and opened it up, there wasn't much left of him. Could there be another way to learn the mummies' secrets? One that didn't involve taking them apart?

For almost one hundred years, the Royal Ontario Museum had had in its collection another mummy — a woman named Djed.

Djed's mummy was housed in a beautiful casket made of linen, papier-mâché, and glue. The case was decorated with Djed's image, and symbols and pictures in gold, red, and orange. It revealed that Djed had been a musician in the great temple of Amun-Re at Karnak. Her husband had been a temple doorkeeper.

Djed's mummy case was one of the best preserved of its period. It was also extremely fragile. It would be impossible to take out the mummy without ruining the priceless case.

The mummy was finally examined in 1994, but no knives or saws were used. Instead, scientists put the case in a CAT scanner — a machine that provides several cross-section X rays of the body, like slices in a loaf of bread. These X rays can then be reconstructed to form a 3-D computer image.

The CAT scan revealed what lay inside Djed's case: linen wrappings, skin and

(Far left) Scientists wondered how they could examine Djed's mummy without destroying the exquisite case. (Left) This wall painting shows female musicians entertaining a pharaoh.

bones, and finally, the internal organs, which had been removed, embalmed, and then placed back inside the body in small packages. Jewelry lay between the bandages: a gold vulture with outstretched wings, and a stone beetle, a symbol of life

The Mummy is Revealed

Placing Djed's mummy case in a CAT scanner (below) allowed Dr. Peter Lewin (left) and technician Stephanie Holowka (right) to unwrap the mummy electronically. (Top, bottom right) Cross sections clearly show the outlines of the case, the mummy's linen wrappings, and Djed's skeleton. (Bottom left) It was clear that Djed's husband could afford to

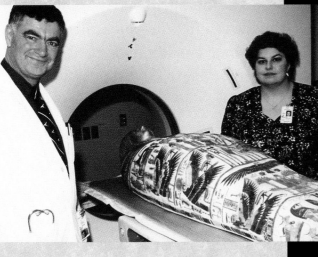

have her mummified by professional embalmers. The CAT scan showed that after Djed's brain had been removed, the empty spaces left in her nose and skull were packed with linen (shown in yellow).

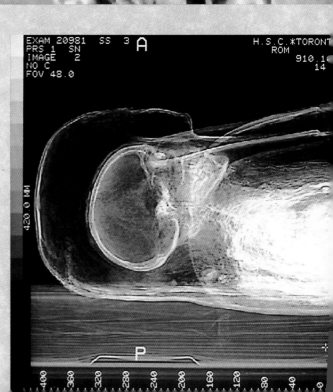

EXAM 20981   SS   3 A
PRS 1   SN
IMAGE   2
NO C
FOV 48.0

H.S.C.*TORONT
ROM
910.1
14

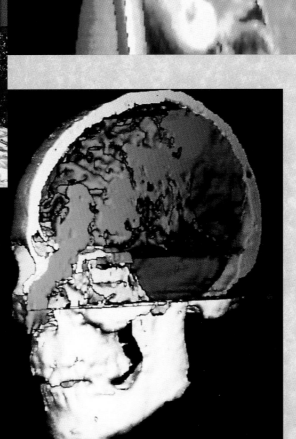

Diets and Dentists

Many ancient Egyptians, including Ramses II, had worn-down teeth. The condition was likely caused by their gritty bread (below), full of sand that had blown in from the desert when the flour was being made (above), as well as the Egyptians' fondness for beer, honey, and other sweet things. The daily meal for many people was bread, onions, and a thick beer. Expensive sweets, like honey cakes, would have been enjoyed mainly by the rich.

Although some historians believe that there were dentists in ancient Egypt, mummies show little evidence of this. There is nothing, for example, to show that teeth were pulled — a logical treatment for someone in as much pain as Djed. Instead, doctors may have drained the abscess with an incision, packed it with dressings soaked in honey, or used alcohol or opium to dull the pain.

after death. A metal plate had been placed near Djed's left hip to cover the incision that had been made during the embalming.

The scan also showed that Djed, though she was thirty to thirty-five years old when she died, had never had children. In childbirth, the pelvic bones shift and then return to their original position. Marks that appear on these bones will show if a woman has had children, and how many.

When scientists viewed the X rays of Djed's head, they could see that small plates had been inserted under the eyelids to prevent the eyes from collapsing and that the nose had been broken when the brain had been removed.

All these things had been seen in other mummies, since they were part of the normal embalming procedure. But when scientists examined the scans of Djed's jaw, they suddenly had a real picture of what her life must have been like before she died.

Djed had terrible teeth. In her upper left jaw was a cavity the size of a quarter. It would have contained a large abscess that may well have burst, spreading infection to her blood, brain, and heart and eventually poisoning her to death. The infection had actually eaten away at the bone, creating several holes.

This abscess would have been horribly painful. Djed's cheek would have been red and swollen. Pus would have drained into her cheek and may even have eaten into the palate at the top of her mouth, affecting her speech.

Djed's cheek abscess was the largest, but there were also more than thirteen smaller ones. Twenty-four of her teeth had been exposed right down to the roots, which would have made eating, and even breathing, sheer agony. Three teeth were missing. They had probably fallen out when her gums had become too diseased to hold them.

Today, when a twinge from one small cavity can send many people scurrying off to a dentist, it is hard to imagine how Djed lived with her pain. Yet poor teeth were extremely common in ancient Egypt. The desert sand blew everywhere. It was in the air people breathed, in the food they ate. Sand was also used to help grind flour. Over the years, eating gritty bread would wear down the surface of the teeth, leaving the sensitive root painfully exposed.

Many Egyptians had dental problems, but it was sometimes worse for the rich. They could afford the sweets that all Egyptians loved so much.

The CAT scan gave scientists unique insight into Djed's life and death. In fact, it told them things that an autopsy would not have revealed. An autopsy opens up the chest, abdomen, and skull. But scientists would have to have taken apart the entire face to find the abscesses that the CAT scan showed.

More important, this examination left the mummy intact. Today, the case is as beautiful as ever, and Djed's mummy lies undisturbed inside it.

The Face of Djed

Using CAT-scan images of Djed's skull, artists have reconstructed a picture of what she may have looked like. A computer-imaging expert reconstructed the mummy's face by electronically smoothing the lines of the scanned 3-D image, and defining the eyes, nose, and mouth (near right). Museum officials also asked a police artist to do a portrait using old-fashioned pencil and paper. Using the CAT-scan image as a base, she drew on information about what modern Egyptians of Djed's age look like to sketch in the facial features (center). Finally, she added hair, makeup, and jewelry (far right) based on evidence about hairstyles and clothing from ancient Egyptian art and literature.

The Story of Djed

Sometimes the pain was just a dull throbbing in her left jaw. At other times, it was so sharp that tears came to her eyes and she cried out — when she ate or when she touched her cheek as she adjusted her wig or outlined her eyes with green paint. Even after she spat away the foul taste in her mouth, she could tell that people recoiled at the smell of her breath. Soon she was ashamed to open her mouth.

She had tried every treatment available: packing her mouth with cloves, taking opium when the pain was really bad. The doctor had suggested compresses soaked in honey, but they felt like hot knives being plunged into her jaw.

Yet the gods had been good to her in so many ways. The family's barley and date crops had been plentiful. Djed had a spacious home on the outskirts of Thebes. She loved to lounge in her courtyard, watching the brightly colored window hangings sway in the river breezes, smelling the sweet lotus blossoms from her gardens. In the old days, she would order her slaves to bring out a plate of her favorite date cakes dipped in beer. But now, even the thought of them made her wince.

The pain was sucking all the joy out of her life. As a musician at the Great Temple of Amun-Re, nothing gave her more pleasure than to put on her most elegant robes, play her harp and sing with the other performers. Soon the month-long festival of Opet would arrive. It was a celebration so important the pharaoh himself would attend. But now it was becoming agony just to open her mouth to sing. What if she could no longer participate in the celebrations? What if she would never again sit below the huge painted columns of the Great Hall?

What would she be good for then? She was, after all, a middle-aged woman with no children. She had noticed the pity in the other women's eyes as they proudly carried their babies on their hips. Some could even boast of having grandchildren. But Djed and her husband had no son to look after them in their old age or to build their tomb when they died. She did not even have a daughter to whom she could pass on her musical skill, as her mother had passed it on to her.

When Djed died, her husband mourned for months. He ate little and stopped shaving, as was the custom. Though it cost as much as he earned in a year, he paid for a full funeral and a fine painted casket for his wife. He consoled himself with the thought that in the afterworld, at least, her life would be free of pain.

Epilogue

What happens to bodies when people die? Different cultures and countries have different ways of dealing with their dead. In many countries, bodies are cremated, or burned (the word "funeral" comes from the ancient East Indian word for smoke). The Vikings placed their dead in boats, set them on fire, and pushed them out to sea. People who died during long sea voyages were also cast into the sea, where the bodies quickly decomposed. The wreck of the *Titanic* is still considered a gravesite, even though the bodies of those who died in the sinking no longer exist.

Many people still bury their dead — in coffins placed in the ground or in tombs. And many want to preserve the bodies before burial, just as the ancient Egyptians did. In North America, embalming became common during the American Civil War, when the bodies of dead soldiers were preserved before being sent home to their families for burial.

Modern embalming is usually performed in funeral homes, and, in some ways, the procedure is not much different from Egyptian mummification. The body's fluids are removed and replaced by a chemical solution. Stuffings and pads are used to give a more lifelike appearance. The individual is carefully washed, oiled, dressed, manicured, shampooed, and made up to look as attractive and lifelike as possible. Then the body is usually placed in a coffin for family and friends to view and say their last good-byes. Finally, the coffin is sealed and buried.

Unlike the ancient Egyptians, we do not bury our dead with furniture, weapons, and food. But we do often bury people with items that were important to them. A person may be buried in a favorite outfit or holding a much-loved book or photograph. Friends and family gather together to cry and grieve for the dead, but also to celebrate the life that has been lived. At more and more funerals, you'll see friends remembering happy or funny moments, laughing, perhaps serving the person's favorite food, or playing or singing their favorite music.

The ancient Egyptians would probably have approved. The writings, artwork, and buildings that they left behind tell us that they, too, celebrated life. Their mummies show that they often lived with illness and pain, without the benefit of modern medicines and hospitals, sophisticated surgery, or painkillers. Yet they loved their families and

The World of Mummies

Preserved bodies — produced by embalmers or by nature — can be found around the globe. The peaceful-looking mummy above is that of a man who was strangled and thrown into a bog in Denmark more than 2,000 years ago. The lack of oxygen in the bog prevented his body from decomposing. (Far left) This beautifully dressed Inca mummy may have been a sacrifice to the mountain god. (Left) The arms and legs of this Peruvian mummy were folded so that the body would fit into a small bundle. (Right) The cold, dry air of the South American mountains preserved these 500-year-old mummies.

Animal Mummies

The Egyptians also made animal mummies: crocodiles, cats, dogs, fish, mice, bulls, monkeys, birds, and even eggs have been found. Some were given gold masks. Often these animal mummies were buried with the dead to provide food or companionship. Others were offerings to gods associated with that animal. So many animal mummies have been found that it is thought some may have been specially bred to be religious offerings.

fought their battles with pride and gusto. They valued learning, music, art, and dancing. They loved to dress up and celebrate special occasions. In fact, they loved earthly life so much that they expected and hoped that the afterlife would be very much like it.

The Egyptian mummies are remarkable discoveries from a long-ago time, and we are as drawn to them today as mummy hunters were years ago. We are fascinated to see the bodies themselves, to learn all the gruesome details of how they were preserved, to see the priceless treasures that were buried with them.

But mummies can also tell us a great deal about ourselves. Egyptian mummies are the largest known source of ancient human remains. From mummies, we know that these people suffered from heart disease, arthritis, malaria, and intestinal parasites, just as we do today. On the other hand, they did not have many types of cancer. Mummies can help us piece together a picture of human health — how diseases are affected by diet and lifestyle, how they have changed over time, and how they may change in the future.

Once the supply of mummies seemed endless. Now most of the mummies have been destroyed, and there are probably very few left to find. The supply of mummies is running out, just when we have the ability to learn the most from them.

With new technological advances, we can often determine the age of the body, when the person lived, how he or she lived and died. By identifying mummies' DNA structure, we can trace family trees and see who was related to whom. We can even take fingerprints and reconstruct faces using sophisticated computers. And CAT scans, X rays, and other modern technology mean that we no longer have to destroy mummies to learn about them.

When we look at mummies, it is sometimes easy to forget that these were once real people. After they died, they were painstakingly prepared for a glorious afterlife. They expected their bodies to remain in their tombs forever. Mummies were never meant to be unwrapped and viewed by the world.

But mummies are a precious source of information about ancient peoples. They can help us understand ourselves. We know now that if we treat them with care and respect, they may have even more secrets to tell us.

Glossary

abscess: A pocket of pus inside the body caused by an infection.

amulet: A charm or ornament worn as a protection against evil spirits.

archaeologist: A person who studies people from the past and their cultures.

bitumen: A black tarlike substance.

CAT scan: An image made using a computerized axial tomography scan, which produces cross-sectional X rays of a body.

decompose: To decay or rot.

embalm: To treat a dead body so that it will not decay.

gilded: Covered with a thin layer of gold.

jackal: A type of wild dog.

malaria: A disease caused by tropical mosquito bites, which results in chills, fever, and sometimes death.

mummy: The body of a person or animal that has been preserved by drying.

natron: A salt found near the Nile River in Egypt and used in embalming to remove moisture from bodies.

opium: A pain-killing drug made from the juice of poppies.

parasite: A living thing that makes its home on or inside another living thing.

pharaoh: A ruler of ancient Egypt.

resin: The liquid gum that certain plants or trees produce when they are cut.

sarcophagus: A large stone box used to hold a coffin and a mummy.

tapeworm: A worm that lives in the intestines of humans and other animals.

Picture Credits

All paintings and illustrations, unless otherwise credited, are by **Greg Ruhl**.

Front cover: (Top left) Robert Harding Picture Library; (top right) P. Craven/Robert Harding Picture Library; (bottom left) Courtesy of University Health Network © ROM; (bottom right) The Ancient Art & Architecture Collection

Back cover: (Middle) Scala/Art Resource; (right) Museo Gregoriano, Vatican/Art Resource

Back flap: Scala/Art Resource

1: Griffith Institute, Ashmolean Museum

6: Peter Christopher

7: Scala/Art Resource

8: (Left) Werner Forman Archive/Art Resource; (middle) Private Collection; (right) Museo Gregoriano Egizio, Vatican/Art Resource

9: Corbis

10: (Top left) Bristol Museums and Art Gallery; (top right) Mary Evans Picture Library; (bottom left) Erich Lessing/Art Resource

10-11: (Bottom) Erich Lessing/Art Resource

12: Scala/Art Resource

13: P. Craven/Robert Harding Picture Library

14: SIPA Press/Art Resource

15: (Left) The Ancient Art & Architecture Collection; (right) Erich Lessing/Art Resource

17: The Ancient Art & Architecture Collection

18-19: (All) A.D.P.F./Sygma

22: Robert Harding Picture Library

23: (Left) Corbis; (right) Griffith Institute, Ashmolean Museum

24: (All) Griffith Institute, Ashmolean Museum

25: (Left) Griffith Institute, Ashmolean Museum; (right) F.L. Kennett/Robert Harding Picture Library

26: (Top left and middle) Scala/Art Resource; (bottom left and right) Robert Harding Picture Library; (all others) Boltin Picture Library

27: The Ancient Art & Architecture Collection

28: (Middle) George Rainbird/Robert Harding Picture Library; (right) Mary Evans Picture Library

29: (All) Griffith Institute, Ashmolean Museum

32: (Left) Courtesy of University Health Network © ROM; (right) Photograph courtesy of Royal Ontario Museum © ROM

33: (Top) Peter Brand; (left) Private Collection; (right) Werner Forman Archive/Art Resource

34: (Top, bottom left and center) Courtesy of University Health Network © ROM; (bottom right) Courtesy of University Health Network

35: Borromeo/Art Resource

38: (Left) Photograph courtesy of Royal Ontario Museum © ROM; (right) Erich Lessing/Art Resource

39: (Left) Photograph courtesy of Royal Ontario Museum © ROM; (all others) S. Holowka

40: (Top) Giraudon/Art Resource; (bottom) Erich Lessing/Art Resource

41: (Left) S. Holowka; (all others) Photograph courtesy of Royal Ontario Museum © Bette Clark

45: (Top) Richard Ashworth/Robert Harding Picture Library; (bottom left and bottom middle) The Ancient Art & Architecture Collection; (bottom right) Christopher Rennie/Robert Harding Picture Library

46: Private Collection

48: Giraudon/Art Resource

Index

Recommended Further Reading

How would you survive as an ancient Egyptian?
by Jacqueline Morley
(Franklin Watts)

This book answers questions about what life was like for ancient Egyptians, from pharaohs to peasants. Learn what Egyptians ate and drank, what they wore, where they lived, and what they believed.

Eyewitness Books: Mummy
Written by James Putnam
Photography by Peter Hayman
(Stoddart/Dorling Kindersley)

An illustrated survey of mummies from around the world shows the many ways human bodies have been preserved and the treasures they took with them on their journey to the next world.

Mummies Made in Egypt
Written and illustrated by Aliki
(Thomas Y. Crowell)

This step-by-step, illustrated guide to Egyptian mummy making explains how and why the Egyptians took such care to preserve the bodies of their dead.

Acknowledgments

Madison Press Books would like to thank:
Dr. Peter Lewin and Stephanie Holowka, the Department of Diagnostic Imaging of the Hospital for Sick Children, Toronto, Canada; Dr. Nicholas Millet and Cynthia Lee of the Royal Ontario Museum, Toronto, Canada; Kathryn Dean; Edwin Durbin

Design and Art Direction:
Gordon Sibley Design Inc.

Editorial Director:
Hugh Brewster

Project Editor:
Mireille Majoor

Editorial Assistance:
Susan Aihoshi

Production Director:
Susan Barrable

Production Co-ordinator:
Donna Chong

Printing and Binding:
TWP Singapore

Secrets of the Mummies
was produced by
Madison Press Books,
which is under the direction
of Albert E. Cummings.